D0160736

The Girls with Stone Faces

The Girls with Stone Faces

Arleen Paré

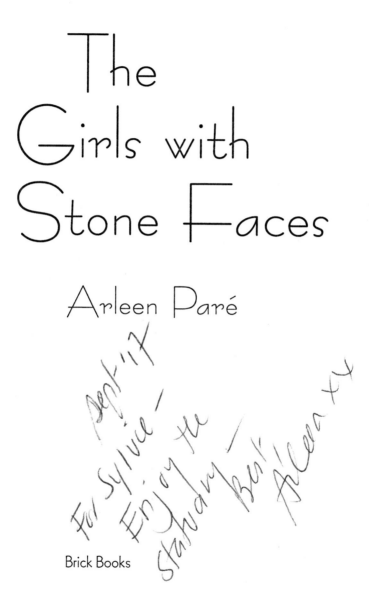

Sept '17

For Sylvie /
Enjoy the
statuary. Best

Arlen xx

Brick Books

Library and Archives Canada Cataloguing in Publication

Paré, Arleen, author
The girls with stone faces / Arleen Paré.

Poems.
Issued in print and electronic formats.
ISBN 978-1-77131-464-0 (softcover).—ISBN 978-1-77131-466-4 (PDF).—
ISBN 978-1-77131-465-7 (EPUB)

I. Title.

PS8631.A7425G57 2017   C811'.6   C2017-902789-1
                                           C2017-902790-5

We acknowledge the Government of Canada, the Canada Council for the Arts, and the
Ontario Arts Council for their support of our publishing program.

The author photo was taken by Ryan Rock.
The book is set in Dante.
The cover image is by Robert Joseph Flaherty, courtesy of the AGO,
Portrait of Frances Loring and Florence Wyle [Church Street, Toronto], 1914; bromide print
(altered with blue tone), 21 × 16.2 cm, 86/116; Gift of the Estates of Frances Loring and
Florence Wyle, 1983
Design and layout by Marijke Friesen.
Printed and bound by Sunville Printco Inc.

Brick Books
431 Boler Road, Box 20081
London, Ontario N6K 4G6

www.brickbooks.ca

For my own dear lifelong companion, Chris Fox

And poetry can also be sculpture,
or at least more like sculpture than it's like conversation.
—Michael Redhill

Florence Wyle and Frances Loring met in 1906 at the Art Institute of Chicago. Florence was twenty-six; Frances nineteen. Both women were deeply in love—with clay. They became close friends immediately. That first meeting they always described as a "click" experience. For almost sixty years, they lived their day-to-day lives, sculpted their neo-classical sculpture, made their living, and built their reputations as prominent Canadian sculptors—together. For most of this time, they lived and worked in a deconsecrated church. They were pivotal in the Toronto art community and were founding members of important national art organizations. Known as "The Girls," their friends included A. Y. Jackson, Fred Varley, Arthur Lismer, and Emma Goldman. Their sculpture is displayed in public art galleries, in parks, on buildings, and on Parliament Hill. They died in 1968 in a nursing home within three weeks of each other and one floor apart.

CONTENTS

First Rooms and . . .

More Room

Room with Rumours, Ruminations

Rooms without Enough Room

Last Rooms

First Rooms and ...

Heart's Arrow

on the ceiling   the Sistine Chapel
that tap   fingertip zap
that divine big bang iconic connection
communion
                by which I mean

art's arrow flies in one direction

you don't change art
it changes you

Arrested Motion: Art, Life

I

as in *Discobolus* the discus thrower levering his right arm elbow up on
an intake of breath the continuous now

II

as in the woman on her way to the store before dinner caught in a down-
pour her sweater now cobra'd over her hair half pound of ground on
the list in her purse three potatoes and one tin of peas stopped in her
rush by the sudden red light her diagonalled body halted midstep while
the purse on her shoulder contrapuntals ahead

III

as in the lava that day in Pompeii leaping into the town into atriums
and vestibulums and the man petrified now the man about to be
stilled reaching in for a piece of fruit in the bowl the bowl being celadon
rimmed with black birds lifting in flight and the fruit five purple-green
figs turning to stone as the man fingers splayed hand

Frances and the Red Velvet Cape

Before velvet: free. Angular free. One hand
tracked only the other
through inside passages of pink granite.
None else could appeal. Before velvet,
tweed. A jacket in wool, the pattern brown-twigged,
regular, knowing the next day will bring the day after.
Worsted always snagged on nail heads and rasps,
unravelled, a line, the hem of a sleeve.
At what cost?
Before velvet she knew little
of cost.
And serge—whenever she knelt to shape clay into toes—
did not soften the press on her knees.
Perhaps a heavy twill skirt, weft equal to warp,
but rarely in red, arterial fire and hood.
Linen yes in the summer but
unshielding. Before velvet: singular. Heart singular. Heart
not yet tuned. A version of free,
cost unconsidered.
Angular, as a falcon angles its wings.
Before velvet she slept alone every night.

Torso 1: The History of Art

after Florence Wyle's *Torso* (*"Mother of the Race"*), c. 1930,
marble, 100.6 cm, National Gallery of Canada, Ottawa

There is, midway, the navel
where once you were hinged
and unhinged
with no recall. There is colour
drained of all colour. Solid
without suggestion of hard.
Resistance
with no hope of resistance.
There is absence: arms, head, legs. No feet
and no hands. There is
        what the world calls beauty.
        Everything isosceles. You
are the code, how beauty is branded.
Gold standard.
Nothing could be more everyday.

In the National Gallery, Room A105

I

thinking of that room
four walls greyish green   the stone in the midst
spacious   almost a shrine   as if a church were assembling itself
from the statuary up   from the mythology already there
without altar or priest
and I
          that day   already halfway in love
as though April had split a sonnet mid-heart
to arrive at the penultimate line

that room in quiet   composed
comprised the *Torso*   the one full of grace
the *Mother* (a name also used) *of the Race*
and *Barrel Maker   Farm Girl   Furnace Girl*
fired black as blue heat
the *Inuit Mother with Child* on her back
and on the west wall another
sculptor's small wooden *Wind* blowing through
the understory   the mute thrall

that day they were all there
maybe even their own girlish heads
their blue plaster busts
blackened bronze *Grief* and the *Sun Worshipper*
erotic   lurching back from her hips
ecstatic as if sun
full on her ebony throat

II

the power of stone   stone standing
or arching its back   or twisting
tilting its hip   looking back
looking over its shoulder
at me

                              those two sculptors
who had mastered plaster and marble
sonorous that afternoon
long dead   they were in the room too
the sounds of the world focussing   finding itself

I was already falling in something like love
a sub-sounding buzz
walking in from the Plamondon two rooms ago
the red-painted nun in bright black-and-white sail
and the three women from Caughnawaga
the small pedestalled bronze
who constantly brazen the storm

walking in as I did up
the stairs   walking in from the atrium   the place of water below
a place once without art
one story up from the Inuit walruses and bears

III

the art in this second-floor room   Room A105
high-polished 3-D
as if inviting   seducing the hand
as if refuge   gardens of cheekbones

haunches elbows and ankles stitchings and caps
rib cages gardenia-white
the room humming a hive full of queens

IV

where I first met their names on the walls
Loring and Wyle
on small careful plaques of smoky green slate
silver-lettered Florence and Frances
the pivotal the key
revelation that
two women
the unexpected

                    amaze

V

those figures wore alabaster they wore blackest black
a formal affair pillared in the way that a church
prescribes formal attire a holy day
some figures wore streaky dove-grey

recollecting chants touching the walls
do not touch do not touch
pale wings power and might
I touched only their names
as if everything here
a reflection
of sky

First Love

Frances studied in both Old World and New, as they say, as if the Earth wasn't carved from one continuous lump, as if the New World could become the Old World made new. Introduced first to blocks of pale clay, tractable, her hands belonging in both. Her mother with her in Europe, her brother too. Her father stayed home though he loved Frances best. Rain and the symbols. Rodin. Paris, Geneva, and Rome. Musée d'Orsay. Cobbled roads. Walls thick as Swiss cows. Buildings that surprised the flat sidewalk stone. Seven years in the old. *The Burghers of Calais, The Gates of Hell.* And yet. The pleasure of mud, reshaping her life. She, too young for real grief. Michelangelo: non finito rising from misshapen ground. *Grief,* she would learn to compose, bending backward and forward, kneeling both ways on the rucked mud, ancient, the old ruinous Earth.

Frances Loved Florence

not reluctant in love Frances loved mud   clay   what you will   first touch
it touched first her fingers   smote the tips   smitten   first love and last
feathered grey earth   sparrow-brown   robin-breast red   skeining her
knuckles   her palms cupped   the cool heft   yielding   but when fired
unyielding as stone

        not reluctant   she loved granite and marble   silica   dry
silica or wet in a paste   she loved cigarettes too and Emma Goldman when
one year Emma came for a visit   and the seven hens with the names of the
seven men who painted mountains and lakes   she loved Delilah the Great
Dane despite the dog's dangerous moods   and Osgood the car   she loved
certain pens   and scaffolds   sitting or standing   leaning out   leaning in
unsafe in the air over pavement and trucks

        arrested motion she loved   the
discus thrower   the way life is almost always about to take flight   the
concept of time unable to catch up with itself   and radio shows   and
meetings   she loved being boss   phone calls and her red velvet cape
more than one glass of scotch   and Florence   oh yes   she loved Florence

Chicago: At First Sight

the moment they meet   morning   classes beginning
end of September when leaves begin day-glowing red
and gold flecks the crazy blue air   each spotting the other
(hell why not use the cliché)
                              across the wide crowded room
high walls and white and wood planks on the floor
the bustle   the enshrined plaster dust
a whiff of dry riverbed   sheets of shale
tall windows mirror the movements of students
Frances Florence
even before they meet face to face   sense
the rasp of stars as if stars are mere cogs
wheels within wheels
how Orion unbuckles
                        and the Pleiades
for once clear as seven clear bells
the solar system resounding   the zodiac   they can hear
its mechanisms of tumblers and locks
brass hoops   keys on a belt   clicking

both of them   falling
                          falling
into that bright frightful place
into the time when sun equals night
all things returning   old turning new

which is what they will tell the rest of their lives
the moment they met

The National Gallery: Unguarded I Would Have Caressed Every Surface

when I walked into room A105   unaware   I knew nothing there   not the
art nor the women nor the women's place in the art   I must have walked
through the room in years past
but this time I was

        struck   stuck   pinned to the air   suspended

                if I could have I would have stroked
every surface   but   there was a guard at the door   I knew only distillate awe
a welter of bliss

I could only memorize the shapes   sanctified   the room a basilica   a concrete
space that transcended the concrete

            each statue a prayer

On the Way In, Three Woman in Bronze

after Marc-Aurèle de Foy Suzor-Coté's *Caughnawaga Women*, 1924,
bronze cast, 43.3 cm, National Gallery of Canada, Ottawa

The three walk into grace. Fierce.
They walk into a gale, heads down, shawls bracing their backs.
Bronze safeguards their bundles
on their way to
or from home. I hope they're on their way home.
Against all odds, rushing there,
tacking their bodies against the history of storm.
They walk into time across scattered fields, along gravel-spiked roads,
over bridges, as if they are Carmelite nuns,
contemplative. In a state of continual speed.
The nature of diagonal is optimistic.
The fired metal they wear reflects black, reflects light.
Altogether they have seven children.
They carry corn, playing cards, cartons of Lucky Strike cigarettes.
One carries a knife.
                       I do not expect them
to meet my eyes. They are on their way,
witnessed on Sherbrooke Street and on Sussex Drive.
In air-controlled rooms they won't stop. I do not expect them
to pray for me.
                    The first white man's world war has come to an end—
so many dead. In the oncoming wind other wars pitch,
battles tighten, tumplines across each woman's head.

Outside the Room in Two Dimensions

after Antoine Plamondon's *Sister Saint-Alphonse*, c. 1841,
oil on canvas, 90.6 × 72 cm, National Gallery of Canada, Ottawa

In her fire-red chair with its carved maple arms, Sister Saint-Alphonse
perches, independent of the chair's back. Her lips purse
as though she has something to say, indulgent,
perhaps indulged as a child, but still,
sadness, a strain round her eyes.
A dignified bird, glorious, underpainted in brown,
cocked a bit left, a bit forward, as if trying to approach
whoever approaches. Nothing judgmental
except for her habit: black robes and a white guimpe,
stiff as the canvas she's painted upon,
which cuts across her young chest above the heavy gold cross.
She does not know the gold's provenance.
She is in all places pyramidal, even her two fingers, index and second,
which hold open the red leather missal, in triangulation, at the right page,
the fingers forced: at the base, the web of skin
stretched over-wide. For hours. She smiles almost
and light radiates from behind her plush chair.
There is crimson. And light.
There is black and white strain.

Florence's Father

Father Wyle was the father
who bent over his daughter's bed in the night
to adjust her small body in sleep.
She was unable to read the clock
shaped like a barn on the shelf in her room.
Or any clock. She was not yet of an age
to read clocks.
And darkness had spread
over her head like two over-large wings,
slurry or coal dust
or mud.

Frances's Father

Father Loring was the father who broke into the house in New York, once a stable, when no one was home, having sent the two women away to care for his aunt ailing in the Midwest. He had a strong will; it was his desire to leave the two women bereft. He emptied their home—a fairy-tale father, a fairy-tale plot. It is not quite right to say that he pillaged, but the fourteen-foot angel was not seen again. Nor his daughter's silver hairbrush. Nor the long strands of her hair webbed in its bristles, each one a dark shimmer. It is not quite right to say he wished them bereft. But bent. Yes. Under his wing.

Games in the Inuit Gallery

after Noah Echalook's *Woman Playing a String Game,* 1987, dark-green
veined stone, ivory, hide, 26.1 cm, National Gallery of Canada, Ottawa

The baby on the woman's back
wishes to return to her true home in heaven—
an island just north of Inukjuak. She sings to ghosts
and snow buntings
through her tiny square teeth.
The birds, minor gods, vanish through the room's square metal vents.
She drills her ivory-point eyes at the loss,
and at the overhead lighting, artificial, a meagre replacement for sun.

She believes if she climbs her mother's stone braids,
she will find herself closer.
Her mother pays no attention.
Though she holds her arms wide,
it is not for the baby.

The mother is playing a game.
She loops lengths of pale leather string round the backs of her hands.
She does not care for ghosts or who watches her
as she twists the thin hide, twists her mouth into a grin,
or the weight of the child on her rippled green hair.

Florence and Her Twin Brother

if there is an in to the house
there must be an out

if there are twins
and one is a daughter
fifty-fifty   there might be a son

if there are two
one daughter   one son
even twinned
they will be   divided
the chores too divided between
the one in the house and
the one out
                and the one in
will be she
and the one out will be he

these are the conventions

so it follows that she
whose name is Florence
will be in the house washing floors boiling sheets
but will want to be out
her face to the northern horizon
feeding the fowl   weeding beets

she will be in   as she must be in   but
she will offer to seed scarlet runners
in the side yard near the fence

and he   (whose name is Frank)
already out
will suck blades of grass through gaps in his teeth
as he pleases as he lies
on his back in the field full of corn
largely unseen

while she who is Florence
works both the in and the out   fry pans and trowels
largely unnoticed

and if in this family love is
on offer she will choose the broken
black rooster instead

The Mothers

there were mothers
one for each girl
Frances and Florence
each in their place
but
there was no poison there
at least
not enough

Motherhood

they left it alone
unless you count
the *Mother of the Race*
or the *Inuit Mother with Child*
unless you count
the stray cats
or the stone babies
crouched on the studio floor
with their stiff granite lips

The Babies

those babies left home before they could walk
though they never would walk
before they were weaned
though they never sucked
paid for and wrapped
oh yes
        those stone babies were loved
patted   rubbed to a sheen
incandescent they were
cheeks burnished black
polished white

Torso 2

after Florence Wyle's *Torso* (*"Mother of the Race"*), c. 1930,
marble, 100.6 cm, National Gallery of Canada, Ottawa

considering you   *Mother*
of the whole human race   past   present
whatever comes next
Jeanne d'Arc   her impossible stance
and Edith Cavell   Pussy Riot   their faces
too young on the screen   not giving up
Rosa Parks   Harriet Tubman's stout trust
considering yours   as if you are
holding your breath   taut
as if teaching the right way to stand
demonstrating how to persevere
each rib accounted for
each muscle   belly   buttock
shoulder to hip   tipped   the whole
on a slight turn   the shoulders
on an almost imperceptible slant
your skin like dolomite marble
shadowed   opening to light
how you mean to safeguard   protect
even though you lack
eyes   ears   lack
a whole human face

Frances Recalling How Florence

the clouds too were young   and the building's exterior stairs   limestone
swirling pink   swirling grey   the slap of soles on the treads   the students
their hair pinned into place and their long cotton skirts hemmed with dust
their white bunchy smocks

recalling the click   how Florence   becoming legend that day   that very
second   through the door   the wanton shock
                        her hair piled with combs and tortoiseshell clasps
almost toppling off to one side   her hands white as though she wore lace
gloves past her wrists   her eyes   determined   black knives

Florence Loved Frances

Reluctant and yet
                    Florence did love. Had loved
the black rooster, had loved the wind rough
across blue Midwestern plains, meteorites
slashing out of prairie night skies.
The northern lights. The thought of. Violet
and shape-shifting green.
And cats, all cats in all places, she loved.
Her grey suit; she admired its shapely lapels.
Ancient Greece, of course,
beauty and truth, her attachment:
don't mess with a column of unbroken strength.
Carving away extra flounce,
she loved unadorned. The unadorned female form,
she loved and was smitten. Despite or because of the breasts.
Frances, while often adorned, berets and broad skirts,
was of female form. She loved Frances too.

First Home

they first lived together in the dead end   MacDougal Alley at number 6
with Frances's mother   the day of the census in 1910   whose name was
Charlotte but   did Charlotte stay in New York for more than one day   in
the stable   and if yes   why and how long   this is mere curiosity   as if
events could be laid out and explained

they were young "sculptors working on their own account" meaning no
identifiable jobs   April so the air must have smelled of new grass and dung

the reference letter from Taft whom Florence had spurned   accused them
lovers he called them   he called them too close   unfit for teaching   for the
jobs they thought would be theirs

heart of Greenwich   heart of their hearts   smitten   coach houses and
poets   political tracts   free spirits   sex   a colony there   bohemia scenting
the loud urban air

they posed for each other   surprised each other's faces in precise states of
patience   or longing   plaster casts patina'd plain Krishna blue   braided
their hair blue round their crowns   to keep it out of the orange and green
clay   their collars draped round their necks   unwary   too loose to inspire
faith that real jobs will arrive

the stable already converted   ceilings   high rafters   suited for their
soaring art   the die cast   the horses   already out of the barn

Having Been Made to Abandon Their Lives

In the photograph the two sit
gazing left, to the east, composed in that way,
profiled in kimonos and loose-knotted scarves.
They've been removed. Are they forsaken?

The Pool Angel, appalled, had spread its wings,
escaped through the high stable roof.

Come to Toronto
(the father's telegram read).
Stop. *Take the ten o'clock train;
do not return to New York.* Stop.
Greenwich Village. Stop.
*Your lives
have been rearranged. What is there in life that won't disappear?*
Stop.
Stop. *Do not regret the loss of your lives in that place.* Stop.
*Or the Angel with its wings wide as a dray horse
nose to tail.*

Technicalities of Neoclassical Sculpture in the Beaux Arts Tradition

Florence was exact; Frances, just a little bit brash. Together
they cast their lot, checking for flaws, flecks, bubbles,
imperfections that must be removed.
As opposed to life—
imperfections in life must be borne.

Point, line, and depth: these form the dimensions of sculpture.
There is a fourth, which is time, elastic, supple,
hard to predict, the classical
always trying to flatten it out.
As with Florence and Frances,
the time there between them, the point,
the line, and the depth.

Plastic, additive, assembling. Subtractive too, a carving away.
The process working in either direction.
Between the two women.
With plaster, there are multiples, mould-making, indexical,
seeking out each intentional detail. Plaster casting:
the benefit of many from one.

From instinct alone, they fashioned maquettes. Sketches.
Clay models, half-size or life. How much they loved
clay. Their own lives added to
and subtracted. Their studio, their home in one place.
They draped damp sheets over the clay,
the half-finished figures studding the room,
not to crack.

To cast first in plaster, the liquid pour left to set.
To reinforce, chicken wire or burlap, each other,
their lives in the church.
They learned to apply
armature, their life a crucible,
lead wire or wood, wire mesh to protect.
A form of fibre after the first coat of plaster is spread.
If waste, they chipped it away. If piece, they disassembled.
In either case they learned loss.

First cast, for shows and exhibitions;
inhibitions, they kept to themselves.

How well-paired for this art,
how singular each was in her being.

To release the clay model, to leave negative
impressions inside the mould,
or the mind. Mother mould. Learned to love
the idea
of negative space, lost wax or sand casting.
Lost wax into bronze—the foundry's blistering heat—
the wax completely burned out.

To be unafraid. To embrace height. Frances
on loose boards over cars
and the dark tops of fedoras.
And weight, to embrace giant blocks of stone,
cold weather and heat, the extremes,
whatever was hard and unyielding.

To use files to smooth and to soften: riffles, rat tails,
flat bastards, and sometimes, the half-round.

Their own personal tools, they carved
from apple wood and cherry, small shaping tools, customized,
wire loops with wood handles to lift out,
gouge what was refractory, unneeded and spare.

Patinas, encrustations or film—
to display a suitable surface—
green to signify bronze, terracotta for stone.
They learned sealing wax and shellac,
linseed or paint to preserve.

To select the best foundry.
The most expert stone carvers: Italian,
in the state of New York, who worked from the full scale,
rough-cutting the stone block leaving a mere quarter inch
for the Girls to refine.
The final cuts. How deep an ear. How round an eye.
Surface, refinement, high-shine or matte.
How much a pink marble mouth
must lift at the left corner,
almost into a smile.

More Room

November 27, 1920, *Toronto Daily Star*, Arts News

Miss Florence Wyle and Miss Frances Loring have been obliged to vacate their old quarters on Church Street (big city news) and had difficulty in getting any new studio with ceiling sufficiently high to admit their big pieces of sculpture (as if they would house anacondas, elephants, giant panda bears). They finally secured an old church not in use and are fitting it up for combined studio and dwelling.

They are moving, yes, fitting up the old church, becoming renowned. Daily news. But the road to this church on the far side of town is not fully paved, too far for patrons and friends, for the custom of art. In time, they'll buy an old farm farther north out of town for larger figures and heads. They have little money, but that isn't news. For now, despite impossible travel, they entertain painters, a few sculptors, certain friends, serve them dinner, serve them news from this satellite edge. They are obliged: who hasn't had difficulty locating themselves, tribulation, something in life that's not quite secure.

This Church Is a Ghazal

They hallow their life in this church,
stumble over clay feet and empty arms in the night.

Where hides the hammer, the two-handed rasp,
the cold hollowed cups, lilies waiting for rain?

Everything they grasp obtains from the earth.
Even the sky overhead casts dust into clouds.

This church is a ghazal; dreams shape the veined stone.
They force thunder through the boards of once sacred walls.

Do they wake in wholeness into each other's arms?
Does the sun dash cobalt, shards of red, gold on the spread?

Florence: Day by Day

all their days they are in
conversation in the same rooms
verso con verso
first is the morning and whether the weather
one side or the other
the shape and landscape of rain in November
cats and dogs
the way the front door continues to stick
this time of year every year
preventing entry
of neighbourhood children
patrons and hens
but when the white winter sun
slides over the hedge
the kitchen door will not catch
will not even close

        in the afternoon
peeling the Gravensteins
Frances admits
she has poured sour milk
into the dish for the fourteen feral cats

Frances: Day by Day

every day one place or another   contrapuntal   warp and weft
conversational rhythms and spikes   morning and Florence mumbles and
Frances cannot remember   all day her dream lies in wait   a bird perhaps
in the Avoca ravine or the Yellow   or the dead poet   the mother of lyric
with a raw fragment of nose   or she might have been walking the dogs
the dogs barking at nothing   pitching themselves through the bracken
brambles that overtake the steep slope   the edge of the path

Frances will tell Florence about losing the dream   Florence says the wind
has its own voice

Frances calls the committee   no one answers   dreams will return   she
does not need to recall what was said   dreams recur and recur

Frances considers the leashes   her purple beret   the sun has not yet
pierced the low cloud   rain still leaks from the eaves

Torso 3

after Florence Wyle's *Torso* (*"Mother of the Race"*), c. 1930,
marble, 100.6 cm, National Gallery of Canada, Ottawa

what I love about you
is the way you
shift your left leg to the fore
as though making a point
though you have no left leg
nor a right   only
a fierce suggestion
of leg   suggestive of pillar
prerogative   without dispute
unendable   a political stance   clear
comfort   confrontational
in this neoclassical room   a swagger
your spirit unassuming
perhaps unintentional
intuiting Eros
the way your navel speaks to your lower centre of gravity
its gravitational pull
foundational   a gravitas centralis
serene at the place
seven fingers below a small frangible bone in the peak of the cage
your breasts small and no-nonsense
I love your two unheavy breasts
also your neck
which is partial
your collarbones
the spread to your shoulders
implying two perfect arms
though no arms exist

unwinged and
                    no head rises above
I love your clear mind   forked lightning
cliffs of white chalk   belly of bone

The Group Poses Stiffly

after a domestic photograph in *And Beauty Answers*,
photographer unknown

the two artists sit in their black and white church patient in the silver
gelatin print   facing the camera as do their twelve plaster casts   other casts
wait out of the frame   a small crowd of their own   the flash will signal
the end   the two women will then rise to thank their stone and cast family
over the years loyal but changeable

Rooms with Rumours, Ruminations

Torso 4

after Florence Wyle's *Torso* ("*Mother of the Race*"), c. 1930,
marble, 100.6 cm, National Gallery of Canada, Ottawa

You could rise on a thought,
O *Mother of the Race,* how material/
immaterial you are, so far from sorrow.

I write this from another millennium,
from an island in the Triangulum Galaxy.
Lotteries of desire. Eyes seeing
what eyes are taught to call faultless.
What I love about you, salt flats,
fleur de sel, half shells on the grey shore,

is how you
        love me back. All this is true:
you can rise in an updraft,
assumpted, with no assistance at all.

Florence Sets Her Compass

She was always heading north from Illinois State.
No north was ever quite north
enough from her Waverly roots.
Or from Chicago
where she first learned to cut infant fingers and thumbs.
Heading north even then. North
being as away as away could possibly be.
Even New York. Always
in that boreal aim, hair to her waist
when she left, gleaming black ice.
Most places, too warm.
To Toronto. In Toronto
she cut her black curtain hair. Determined—
she never fit in. From Toronto
she had a clear shot at the pole.

No Sidesaddle Beauty

She straddles the bench, boots blunt on the floor.
The knife in her hand, a penknife, sharp
shining steel, sharp
as the woman's right eye,
slices away at the lower half of the baby's wet ear.
Her apron is canvas, clotted with clay, grit,
mud of the day, damp parings the size
of sow bugs or the wings of a fly.
The apron, her hair, her trousers, all dunnish grey.
She slices the spot where the baby's ear
bridges the baby's lined skull,
the spot where the small lobe perfects its pendulous curve,
almost unweighted, unfixed.

Across the room, which is not an over-large room,
another woman
masses in her deep velvet chair.
With her left hand, she cradles the black phone,
casts her eyes to the woman
who whittles in the baby's fine face.

A kind of love,
                    deliquescence,
permeates this space.

In her right hand,
the morning's fourth cigarette.

Say

after Laurie D. Graham's "Rove"

say terracotta   say this dense complication of earth   say dirt
say mud the colour of rust   say clay   dry stone   say dry riverbed
say river   bed with old springs   open the windows in mid-July
say plaster is stone   with or without pigment applied
limestone   calcified   say granite is igneous
say biceps hard as petrified wood
say future is harder than past
tip of the iceberg   say tongue
gravity   symmetry   multiverse   say holes
in sculptural art have no part
in or out of the torso
say holes do not belong in a column of stone   upright
or in recline   say classic   say the core holds
smooth as the Tiber at night   say tongue
touch   greed   say I want   say
I want patina   smooth as a mirror   a mother's breast
a keen hunger for satin   to handle   say silk   silky nature   say
between the two thighs   surface
surface tension   say arrested motion
meniscus   say spill   say palms oiled in sweat
say opposable thumbs   fingers
tips as knowing as a black ant's antennae
sonar   bat wings   knowing as photons   as smell
knowing as bodies in summer's impossible
heat   say nipples   eye to eye
say
      come over here

Magnetic North

when she left the church
unsanctified   on her way
sky blighted   grey studded with grey   the northern limits of grace
the city already taut   the limits now out of reach
roads   where there were roads   mudded over
end of the bus line twelve blocks ago

how would she return

leaving Frances well before breakfast
walking   hoping for more than tundra
cuticles stuffed with rock flour
fingers chiselled almost to bone

more than salvation

her boots the boots of a man
made for distance and scree
and her hat
her pants the pants of a miner   a machinist

her future   the northern limits of light

when did she renounce the world's judgment
start to focus so hard
on the approval of stone

The Lure of Light

after Davidialuk Alasua Amittu's *The Aurora Borealis Decapitating a Young Man,* 1965, dark-grey stone with brown veins, 23.2 cm, National Gallery of Canada, Ottawa

A legend must be exact.
A lesson, a terror, the angles of stone cut with fastidious care.
A pulsating glow.
If you purse your lips.
If you. On any night, if you blow while the sky. Sky
rummaged with violent intent, parlous thrall,
rivering green, neon mauve, white slides, slashes,
captivates bubble-gum pink.
If you feign. If. The colours, the movement alone.
If you open your mouth.
On any night.
If you think you are better
than light, the sinuous flow. You.
Your arrogant head. Lose it.
Beheaded. You. Your pride.
Cradled, stillborn, your head
in the crook of your hapless right arm.

Her Name Was Ana Mangurin

after Frances Loring's *Inuit Mother and Child*, 1938, carved 1958,
limestone, 193 cm, National Gallery of Canada, Ottawa

The child on her back sees something the mother can't see.
The mother knows something we cannot know.
What I see are rows of small scars in the folds of her sealskin dress.
Or are they scars? Or is it a coat, tunic, an apron?
The coat, or the apron, drapes into the fold between the tops of her legs.
I see stone flushed pink. With mannered marks,
tight rows that a chisel has made.
Not the cold. Not the limitless snow.
I don't see the long dark in November.
Nor the lip of a life paused
          before everything, snow, apron
          or amauti,
          sealskin or scars,
walked into modernity.

Her name is Ana Mangurin. She lives not far from Frobisher Bay.
But the child?
What we can't see is what the child sees,
where she will go.

Florence's Compass

some nights she did not leave their shared bed
some nights she did not even walk down the stairs
did not leave their shared room
or leave the house that faced east
or the street that ran north
or the city that spread like spidered ink on a map
some nights
she sank into the groove in the bed that ran south
that the years and both bodies had made
lying in the same north/south direction
the groove on those nights brimmed
with them both   the bed was not wide
vast heat brimmed over the sides

Matters of Taste

do you care for their sculpture
the woman asks me at the patio party
glass of wine in her hand
she can't hear   she reads lips
so I nod   mouthing yes   I say
yes   I like their work   but
because of the question   how it's asked
in that moment I begin
to understand there's another
more acceptable answer
even now it's understood
their art is considered passé
neo-Greco-Roman outmoded
pretty perfection
no avant-garde holes   the hollows
of Hepworth and Moore
to penetrate the middle
of things
removing the core
holes where a heart can fall through

but still I
nod   shape the word
yes
                and were they
lesbians   do you think

I nod again   mouth the word
obvious   they were lovers
perhaps of the classical bent

Rooms without Enough Room

On Relief in the Thirties

from Relief there is no relief
not last year not this
always oats in the morning
whether rain glazes the windows
or snow measures the sill
or house flies
silt the corners where putty fights frost
and powdered milk   always
potatoes at noon   mashed
some days   depending
or baked in their own scabrous skins
and eggs   always eggs
from the chickens that peck the backyard
or there might be sardines   cats licking the tins
tongues risky on the razor-sharp lids
or pressed meat in squares   saltines
at 8:30 with cubes of pale yellow cheese
on Relief
                    and on Sundays   a stew
perhaps chicken with turnip or leeks

no one is starving   no   who can complain   but
never humbugs or chocolate or white mints in a bag
no steak or half-decent scotch
no good tea or biscuits with jam
no relief   and who will
but Florence
complain

How Heavy Art 1

Too heavy on days in November
on the scaffold over the highway,
limestone, the over-large lion,
traffic speeding under the boards. Frances,
the weather weighting her shoulders,
her gloveless hands, the groan
of the planks as she shifts
her hips, the slip
of the chisel in sleet,
the soft place between index and thumb,
sleet icing her hair, feet hanging
over the traffic, thirty feet up, the lion
safe on the ground
looking up from below, the sudden
urge to cut into the animal's cheek.

How Heavy Art 2

Knowing its unarguable weight, The Girls chose not
to weigh art, not its costs, nor its time,
the displacement it caused every day,
nor did they bother to count the eggs the hens laid;
they left their purses in the spoon drawer
with the old rasps and rings.

To Age in New Light

If she walks following Yonge Street,
leaving the line of St. Clair, past city limits, street lamps thinning out,
people giving way to foxes, feral cats bawling,
ruts, tufted grass, sumac, purple deep in its heart,
past where black-and-white cows gather,
each one an erratic shy stone if she squints,
visors her hands as she passes by
as if she's a god with two feet,
not pausing
not even to scrub her chipped nails or the fine lines that pucker her knuckles,
not for sleep, not to allow herself to rest on her left side or right,
for fear
of her father who made her sleep on her back as a child.

She is small—twinned from birth. The future
recedes, is reduced even as she walks north. No comfort in new.
If she flies, keeps her head,
if the aurora could lift her
past arboreal forests, snow carved with wind.
Limned as autumn becomes a new winter,
ends of worlds chiselled out.

She is humble, too old to learn very much new.
Nor does she care.

She will miss Samson, Delilah, Peter the Great,
each headless torso, the bronzes,
the queen of her life. She carries her mallet and knife.

Unrelinquishing of original purpose,
a question of will.
Those lights, borealis, will pull thoughts from her mind,
air from her lungs, empty her out.
She is grateful.
They will shake the whole sky.

Under Glass

in this cornered space
public   in this alcove among what is left
their two faces
unsmiling   west-facing
inside the glass case they inhabit
not meeting each other's eyes
secluded   with a fine scrim at their backs
backs to the wet springtime street
umbrellas   maple leaves
unfurling a new rotation of green

Identity

we are cats among chickens

                    racoons at the back door

bindweed   horsetail   buttercup
gout

                    hollyhocks mid-July

we lived in a stable

                    no horses   no horseflies   no sheep

we live in a church

                    no blessings or prayers

we eat in a studio

                    we sleep up the stairs in an old vestry bed

statues   reliefs and half figures

                    strays   bowls of coins

we talk to each other

                    we listen through snow in the backyard

neighbourhood children call us
clay ladies

                    their fathers might call us some queer

pull in your ears   I call you
queenie

                    I call us clever   I call us first-rate

ordinary as two cups
of orange pekoe tea

        steeped black as pools underground

we are famous

       then presto—

            completely unknown

How Art Works

It's not that they will die.
They *will* die: early winter and a revolution
already rummaging the streets. Nineteen sixty-eight,
three weeks, one woman, then the other,
black holes, infinities, their bones, bare,
blue puckered skins. It's not that. That
they can accept.
It's not that they have not rattled pain
for years. Between them.
Or seared their joints
or lost their thoughts or teeth or hair
or words that catch between the pages of their minds.
All this they accept and do not fault.
It's not the money, not having cash or sufficient
bank accounts, coins clattering the small porcelain bowl
on the table near the front door.
It's not the friends who die. Are dying. It's not the shoes
that warp at heel and pocket on the outer sides. The faded coats.

It's Henry Moore,
the holes he sculpts inside their minds, their bodies, art,
their peace. The way his art will leave theirs behind.

They Hated His Monsters 1

after "Terror and Beauty," the Francis Bacon / Henry Moore exhibit,
Art Gallery of Ontario, Toronto, 2014

everything in the world of form is understood through our own bodies
— Henry Moore

including   trauma   second world war   Elephant and Castle   the tube
station there   the women in London sleeping nights through the war
huddled on the underground floor while bombs in the streets overhead
full moon or new   they would raise themselves on their elbows   haunches
and palms   the grievous strain   their chins tilted up as if the ceiling could
interpret the night   reclining figure   plaster casts her eyes to beseech
speechless   two-piece prone figure waits for arms   for any news of

His Monsters 2

after drawings from Henry Moore's "Shelter Sketchbook," 1940–1941, pencil, wax crayon, coloured crayon, watercolour wash, pen and ink on off-white lightweight wove, 204 × 165 mm, "Terror and Beauty" exhibition, Art Gallery of Ontario, Toronto, 2014 (courtesy of The Henry Moore Foundation, UK)

In the human figure one can express more completely one's feelings about the world than in any other way
— Henry Moore

the trains emerged from the tunnels   dark holes in the undergroundscape
monstrous mouths   the air above screaming as they propped themselves
on their hands keeping track of the bombs   bracing themselves against
the assault   ten thousand people   more   on platforms under the city
bunkers   distortions   sketches dismembered   voids   sockets and gouges
figures   one eye like a squid   breastbone of a bird   sparrows dart through
seated woman   fragmented   pushing herself up   pushing   draped woman
whose reclining body the size of a small car   whose head a tight fist
pushing herself up into a blade   scapular

Torso 5

after Florence Wyle's *Torso* (*"Mother of the Race"*), c. 1930,
marble, 100.6 cm, National Gallery of Canada, Ottawa

fragmented form   unfinished sentence
foundational object seeking
new foundational space
seeking change   a red velvet cape   a grey suit
a pair of kid gloves
subjectification   a way to start over
propose the nautilus as code
a new standard of beauty

choose the peacock
choose panther or koi

His Monsters 3

after Henry Moore's *Seated Figure on Ledge*, 1977, bronze, 26 cm, "Terror and Beauty" exhibition, Art Gallery of Ontario, Toronto, 2014 (courtesy of The Henry Moore Foundation, UK)

I have been more interested in the female form than in the male   Woman *has that startling   fullness of the stomach and breasts   The smallness of the head is necessary to emphasize the massiveness* ...
— Henry Moore

on the ledge
seated figure on the ledge misses her bronze feet
her foundry-hard ankles hang
in the gallery air
downcast
how is she monster   she has lost her talent
to speak

His Monsters 4

after Henry Moore's *Seated Figure: Armless*, 1955, original plaster, 45.6 cm,
"Terror and Beauty" exhibition, Art Gallery of Ontario, Toronto, 2014
(gift of Henry Moore, 1974)

the seated figure is armless
her stiff shirt billows with distortions of fear
circular incisions   an inflexible fashion
nor does she have ears
one arm has been torn off at the shoulder
the other at the mid-bicep
nor is there a mouth
yet she asks
entreats

Two Factory Girls Carry a Rail

after Frances Loring's *Girls with a Rail,* 1918–1919, bronze,
71.1 cm, Canadian War Museum, Ottawa

Just because you wear factory men's shoes does not mean
you are men. Does not mean you will be afforded
the tricks, treats of men.
Just because
you are possessed of four hands,
two work-gloved with flares past the wrists.
Just because. You sport workday pantaloons, just because
you carry a rail, the weight of the war,
just because war warps the rules, the roles,
does not mean
you will not be marooned.
Does not mean you will not be expected.
You are written in bronze, does not mean you will shine.
Does not mean you will be rewarded. Not asked to lower
your eyes, expectations, drop the rail, drop any resentment.
Dropped
back into your kitchens
or streets or small beds at the back of old family homes.
Just because you now knead your own bruises,
muscles, cramps in your calves,
does not mean you cannot knead the bread.

His Monsters 5

after Henry Moore's *Seated Figure Against Curved Wall*, conceived 1956 – 1957, cast 1957, bronze, 56.4 cm, "Terror and Beauty" exhibition, Art Gallery of Ontario, Toronto, 2014 (gift of Mrs. Harry Davidson and family in memory of Harry)

the curved wall where the underground train will appear   where the train
will perform its full sweeping turn   almost shaking the woman seated
against the bowed wall   she doesn't move   expectant   as if   she is talking
to a false face   no one is there

        three-quarter figure   three-quarter figure
        and another   three-quarter figure
        for a long time nothing is whole
        there are spaces
        where once swallows performed

Loring and Wyle: Core Drilling

a strong core of a thing   they wanted   art where the centre would hold   a
core drilling pillared   not something with too many parts protruding or
scooped out or missing   but the centre
but the centre
                    shifted
                              in the typical tectonic way of the world   which
                                    moves to topple   how the Milky Way
loops over and over itself   ourselves   indicates there are no simple centres
only thoughts of centrality   shifting   tipping sideways   each time twisting
through a new (off-) central place   questioning   testing

Last Rooms

All Things Removed

Angels, of course, go missing, stables fall
brick by brick into the street,
frost melts even in the ravines' farthest reaches,
wool coats with fur collars and cuffs, moth eaten, pitted with holes,
plaster busts, gallery stubs washed up in back pockets,
reputations, biographies from library shelves, interviews, an old DVD,
a great niece who lives on the coast.

Is there anything that will not?

Even the room, first day, arrangements
of white, thrilling as icebergs that still convoy
off Newfoundland's coast—
these too will disappear, are disappearing, right now,
crystal by crystal.
The marble torso has been removed,
stone children kidnapped into underground vaults,
black bronzes hauled off before morning light,
their sheen miraged,
merest mark of what was.

Unsure

                 snowflake-white bird in this new month of spring
off course   on its long way long lost   snow bunting butting a fierce streak
of storm   and the door somehow ajar   skiff of snow on the jamb   on the
sill   out of place   as if a loose hem   a scallop of unseasonal frill   the bird
not sure why it is here   the bird late
but

           in this city   here on the sudden high counter considering the table
below   the checkered cloth   what form of perch might be afforded to ac-
commodate the small bird's long spurs on the hind toe of each foot   there
is the handle of a large spoon down from the bowl   recent conveyance
for coagulations of oats   April   and here on the table the cold sun seeps
through fine panes of glass

                 too early for lunch   and yet an instinct for crusts and nubs
of white cheese   despite a clear instinct for places to be   April in this case
means lost   unsure   means left behind

Another *Grief*: Summer Afternoon at the AGO

after Frances Loring's *The Old One,* 1914, bronze, 62.5 cm,
and *Grief,* 1917, bronze, 51.0 cm, Art Gallery of Ontario, Toronto

The Old One will not complain   lonely against the sage-coloured wall
non finito for years   his mood leaching lumpy unpolished into his base
through to the column below   and his pate   smooth as one of Jupiter's
moons   unfocussed   the weight of living too long   everything behind his
unfinished head lies undone

his only kin in the room kneels on a plinth
arching back and yet forth at the same time   blackward her hips   bent
bent on rending her right breast or losing her head into her chest   no one
can see her real face   her anguish prevents it   her heels like two elbows
point to the ceiling   her skirt tied at her waist with a rope   body bronzed
in regret   in slouch kneeling as if she might slide down the rock face   she
is on her way down   being *Grief*

being old *The Old One* averts his world-
weary gaze

Florence: Bracing for Cold

even the polar cap she will reshape
mallet   chisel   two-sided rasp
three pairs of rough gloves lined with wool
shaving the ice to become a small crouch of cat licking its paw
tongue frozen to claw
                      the round polished cold
becoming an infant with its thumb in its mouth
curled round the cap   stylized
almost modern in form
and a woman
rises out of desolate snow
territorial flag
the way a woman might rise
from early years
ends of the earth   crest of the world
clusters of frost flowers riming her lips
the surrounding space crystalline
where her breath   coming easily now
meets the unboundable air

Industry

they left their heads   their bodies   all over the place   they never stopped
making   when one was sold   another was chiselled   another sanded   one
more polished   one more on display   three left the exhibit   they could
hardly keep track   some they left on the faces of banks and big shops in-
side and out   two guarded a highway   they left their own heads in a small
park   a parkette   in an alcove   vaults   the war bronzes they left in the
museum of war   the woman with a stone dish on her shoulder now bends
over the Bain family's fountain   one or two monuments were left on Par-
liament Hill   a foot soldier was left near the ocean   all over the place   they
lost track   in Toronto   St. John   Ottawa and in Niagara Falls   one maybe
two they lost in New York   some left the country for good   some stayed in
private collections   some live on shelves in the basements of galleries   in
numbered cabinets with glass doors and locks

they left their life in the church on Glenrose   got into the car that drove
them away   never looked back

All Things Being Dear

dear *Old One*   dear *Grief*   dear *Mother of the Race* with no head for numbers for counting the children and no hands to hold them dear Inuit mother with one child on her back   dear Ana Mangurin   start of the last century with the same child on her back another paradigm turn   dear bad-tempered dog dear cats who don't belong in the house   dear Florence who did not care for her father but wore his kind of shoes   dear horses who lived in the stable which became the studio which stayed in New York even after they left were made to leave   dear Fred Varley who did not belong in a city or town   dear Dr. Banting dear insulin dear five Banting heads dear neighbourhood children who might be bad children or middling but in any case might turn into doctors or lawyers whether girls whether boys dear clay dear clay ladies dear woolen scarves and felt tams dear order from chaos dear Frances and her red velvet wrap and hooded eyes bedroomed as a barred owl's as the wings of a white luna moth and moonlight dear moonlight   dear scaffolding dear twenty feet in the air   dear snow and snow bunting and snowstorms in May dear men's shoes broken at heel dear A. Y. faithful though art fashions changed dear Vale of Avoca ferns trolley cars struggling up the iced hill dear contradictions of beauty and wrongs   stone rough or stone smooth as ducks' eggs dear solutions if they exist dear Yellow Creek and Mud Creek and brambles frogs willows and mud   muck dear merciful muck

Frances Grew Blind

a small bird perched on her table   its head cocked to one side   in its beak
the word crust   the weather pulled it from one end of the day to the other
morning to night

                                                        at night Frances saw
into her past   past mountains and rivers   traffic   black ice   as a child she
could fly   as a child she swam currents of conversation   their sense nothing
but tone   pulling her morning to night in short spurts   if she could see
the way she once saw   the way a mountain sees into a river   miles away
into the bed of the river   what is strewn on the bed microscopic   wet
worms tiny blue clams   fish scales   nematodes   bits of teeth   the river
sees what lies on its banks   branches   wing feathers   moles   moss   leather
soles   how life begins its slow twist into death
she saw

          the shape of the bird before it arrived   it flew in from the day she
turned nine   a fall day with more tone than cool air   landing now   a ghost
landing   she covered her teacup with her left hand   her mouth with her
right

Beloved of Fingers

remembering that room   remembering
those two who peopled the room with their stone
their stone prevailing   almost turning   raising their heads
those two who recollect blue clay and black
beloved of fingers and palms
their lives moulded
remembering   that room   in the Canadian Galleries   Room A105
those two   days now and days past that flew
through their fingers   palms filled with future
toast on a plate   fragments   jackets and pencils   hair in the sink
bowls of milk skinned with paper-thin ice
bits of poems   strewn through ruins   cities   churches temples
and time   remembering that time
those women who almost cannot remember themselves
their own denouement   their day by day coming apart
almost cannot remember each other's names

I'm Still in Love

three-quarters   halfway
half-in   half-past   maybe four-fifths
the measure is not important
when love enters it clears the blue sluice
clears all imperfections   grey haze   the blind
in the eyes   nighttime
mines the interstices of soul
in love
with these two   the idea of   as if
they almost were one

I tell you this
                         they were gods
nor would they allow the term sculptress
as in less   the gendered hierarchical split
they did not accept less
or allow hunks of clay to be gouged from inside the whole
or allow the trivial   or the absurd or unsightly
these two
and their four hundred works
unsullied
or three hundred seventy-nine
the precise count   unimportant
when love enters it fills more than space or a ledger or time
I'm telling you this
                         these two are deities
                         far back
                         perpetuity

when divinity enters
it enters through the crown chakra
without volition or violence
the top of your head
                          the crown is violet
breaks into sky

Fourteen Lines About Beauty

1. A certain charm informs any numerical system.
2. It's close to beauty, but it is not beauty.
3. A line is only a line, but add a loop, a finale, and you're almost there.
4. It is not the frog.
5. It is not the bog or the weeds or the wart on the frog.
6. Unless you chose the right angle.
7. Philosophers may struggle; apple blossoms pay no attention.
8. If I kiss you, am I more beautiful. Are you?
9. If proportion.
10. If contrast, say blue versus orange.
11. There once were clouds of butterflies. The Italian say farfalle.
12. Papillons in the French.
13. The end might not be beautiful.
14. The beginning. Yes, but middle is best.

Guide to the Plants of Toronto

the year they died
they died together   Frances
and Florence   though apart by one floor and three weeks
that year   the parks in Toronto
waiting at the time   wintertime
when they died
for the plants   for the ferns   flowers   cattails
arum and duckweed   scouring rush
to break through the frost-hardened soil
waiting for the ice to break open
for the soil to go soft as brown sugar
and though neither Frances nor Florence
would have remembered
the names of the plants
plants they had known for the past fifty years
plants growing along the boulevards and creek beds of Moore Park
of Mud Creek and Yellow   on Glenrose and on St. Clair
in their backyard
that year the Botany Group
of the Toronto Field Naturalist Club
produced an olive-green booklet
a checklist of plants in the city
to guide walkers through parks with their children and dogs
life going on without the two women
twigs and beggar's-tick burrs
the way Frances had once walked Delilah and Samson
and some days Florence would walk with them too
ask whether a green shoot might be skunk cabbage
or white or maybe yellow trout lily

and if that yellowish clump might be wolffia or crimson fern
jack-in-the-pulpit they both knew
without doubt

Notes and Acknowledgments

I wish to thank the Canada Council for the Arts for financial assistance with this project. And in no particular order, I would like to thank the following people without whom this collection would not have realized the same level of accuracy: Elspeth Cameron (*And Beauty Answers*, Comorant Books, 2007), Rebecca Sisler (*The Girls: A Biography of Frances Loring and Florence Wyle*, Clarke, Irwin, 1972), and Christine Boyanoski (*Loring and Wyle: Sculptors' Legacy*, Art Gallery of Ontario, 1987), whose texts provided important information about the lives and art of The Girls; Charlie Hill, formerly of the National Gallery of Canada, for discussion and for sending me Christine Boyanoski's catalogue; Christopher Davidson, National Gallery of Canada, for a tour of Loring/Wyle art in the museum vaults; Laura Brandon, formerly of the Canadian War Museum, for contacts; Meredith Maclean, Canadian War Museum, for a tour of Loring/Wyle art in the museum vaults; staff members of the Art Gallery of Ontario for research assistance; John O'Brian, University of British Columbia, for discussion of The Girls and Canadian art; Ann Davis, University of Calgary, for discussion of The Girls and Canadian art; Jessie Jones for her unpublished poem which inspired "Frances and the Red Velvet Cape"; Alice Loring, Frances Loring's niece, for lending me Wyle's chapbook of poetry, *Poems,* and for discussion of her great aunt; Alison Bowes, Alice's wife, who purchased a copy of a CBC *Telescope* DVD so I could view a Loring/Wyle interview with host Fletcher Markle; Maureen Hynes, Toronto poet, who helped with Toronto geography and more; Helen Mills, founder of Lost Rivers Toronto, who helped Maureen with same; the members of the Fiction Bitches and of the Webbels, my two writing groups, who helped with various poems in this collection; Patricia Young, poet and editor, who reviewed an earlier version of the manuscript; Chris Fox, my wife, for providing relevant resource books, support, edits, and more; Donna Sharkey, my sister, for support and for accompanying me to the National Gallery and War Museum vaults, and more; Marsha Arbor, artist, for supplying the term "powdered milk"; Aileen Penner, artist and writer, who loaned me her text on 3-D art; Kathy Ross, who told me everything she knew about the lost wax method; Mowry Baden, sculptor, for a technical discussion on the making of sculpture; Susan Western, once a young neighbour of Loring and Wyle and her brother, Hugh Western, who supplied contacts; Clive and Mary Clark, former Loring/Wyle neighbours, who provided information about the Clay Ladies as neighbours, and took in an abandoned Wyle sculpture that had been discarded as garbage in front of the Loring/Wyle house; Scott James, retired archivist for the City of Toronto, for a discussion at the Arts and Letters Club regarding the sourcing of clay in Toronto. The Michael Redhill epigraph is from *The Globe and Mail*, February 2, 2002. Thanks to the brilliant people at Brick Books, especially Kitty Lewis, Managing Editor par excellence, and Alayna Munce, Production Manager, whose diligence has made this book the most exact artifact it could be. Finally, with much gratitude for his knowledge of poetics, art, and of the Canadian Galleries at the National Gallery, I want to thank my careful editor and very fine poet, John Barton.

Arleen Paré's first book, *Paper Trail*, was nominated for the Dorothy Livesay BC Book Award for Poetry and won the City of Victoria Butler Book Prize in 2008. *Leaving Now*, a mixed-genre novel released in 2012, was highlighted on All Lit Up. *Lake of Two Mountains*, her third book, won the 2014 Governor General's Award for Poetry, was nominated for the Butler Book Prize, and won a CBC Bookie Award. Paré's poetry collection *He Leaves His Face in the Funeral Car* was a 2015 Victoria Butler Book Prize finalist. She lives in Victoria, with her partner of thirty-seven years.